I Remember When ...

Alan Trussell-Cullen

Rigby®

www.Rigby.com
1-800-531-5015

DECLARATION - Page 2

Argus.

The

BRITAIN AND FRANCE AT
WAR WITH GERMANY

BRITAIN'S DECLARATION

"CLEAR"

Rigby Focus Forward

Text © 2006 Alan Trussell-Cullen
Published in 2006 by Nelson Australia Pty Ltd ACN: 058 280 149
A Cengage Learning company

1 2 3 4 5 6 7 8 374 14 13 12 11 10 09 08 07
Printed and bound in China

I Remember When ...
ISBN-13   978-1-4190-3674-3
ISBN-10   1-4190-3674-2

Acknowledgments
Illustrations by Julian Bruère
The author and publisher would like to acknowledge permission to reproduce material
from the following sources:
Photographs by APL/ Corbis, p. 5/ Hulton-Deutsch Collection, p. 11; Australian War
Memorial, p. 7/ 138692, cover, p. 1; Fairfax Photo Library/ Rebecca Hallas, p. 8 top; Getty
Images/ Keystone/ Stringer, pp. 8 bottom, 13/ The Image Bank, p. 12; Coo-ee Historical
Picture Library, back cover, pp. 3, 4, 6, 14.

I Remember When ...

Alan Trussell-Cullen

Contents

THE WAR

I remember World War II. I was going to school.

DECLARATION — Page 2.

Elliott's GINGER BEER MINA WATER

The **Argus.**

LAWRENCE FRENCH DRY CLEANED
One Quality   The Best
SUITS PLAIN FROCKS & COSTUMES

No. 29,027

MONDAY, SEPTEMBER 4, 1939.   12 PAGES   PRICE 1½d.

BRITAIN AND FRANCE AT WAR WITH GERMANY

CHAMBERLAIN'S DECLARATION

"OUR CONSCIENCE IS CLEAR"

FULL SUPPORT

This is my mom,
the new baby, and me.

My dad was fighting in the war.
He had been away for over a year.
Some fathers had been away for over two years.

LIFE WAS HARD

The war made life hard for all of us.

Mom had to have **coupons** to get food at the shops.
People had to stay in line for hours to get food for their family.

coupons

Mom had to work in a factory
making things for the war.

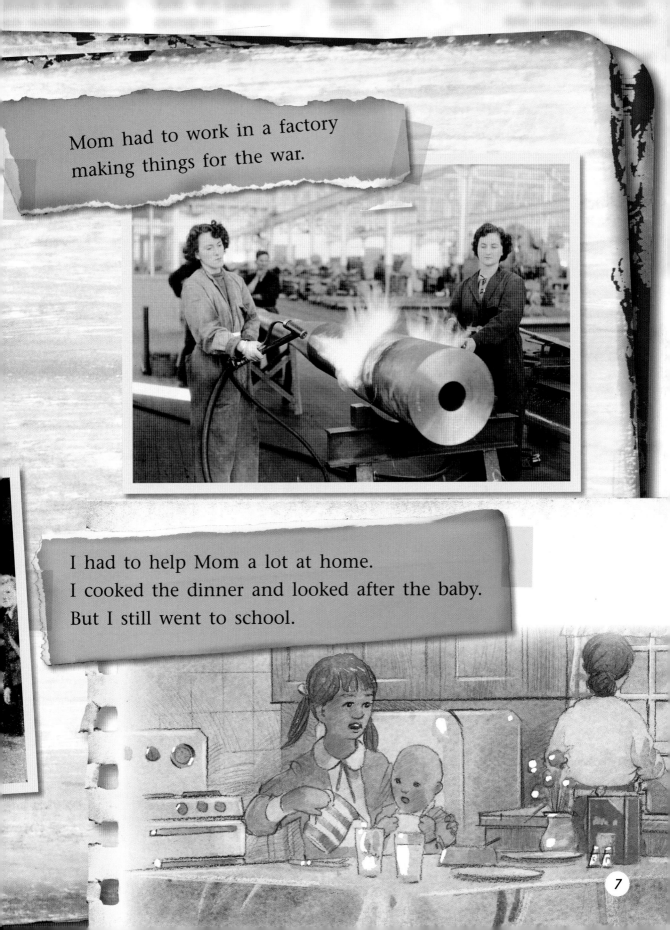

I had to help Mom a lot at home.
I cooked the dinner and looked after the baby.
But I still went to school.

GOING TO SCHOOL

This is my school.

We did our work
on little blackboards.

I walked to school,
but other children rode their bikes.
We did not have a car, and there were no buses.

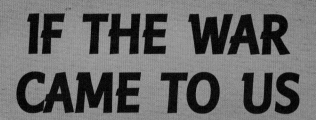

IF THE WAR CAME TO US

Sometimes the teacher made us sit under our desks.
She said this is what we had to do
if a plane flew over the school.

But we were lucky.
No planes flew over our school.
School children in other countries had to hide
in **bomb shelters**.

THE NEWS

At night,
we sat by the radio to hear the news
about the war.

On Saturdays, we went to the movies. Before the movie, they showed **newsreels** about the war.

MRS MINERVA - GREER GARSON
NEWSREEL - THE WAR IN EUROPE
HOP A LONG CASSIDY - WILL ROGERS

TICKETS

GOOD NEWS AT LAST

One day, we heard that the war was over.
We were so happy that we danced in the street.
"At last the war is over!" we shouted,
and we danced into the night.

I remember lots of things about the war.
But the day I like to remember again and again
is when my dad came home.

Glossary

bomb shelters	places to be safe from bombs
coupons	tickets or ration cards that let you get things at the shops
newsreels	short movies about the news
World War II	a time when people all over the world were fighting, from 1939–1945

Index